A Thousand Mountains

with Yet/Still, and Other Works

by
Via Satellite

Timothy C. Reece () Scott Mercado () Drew Andrews

A Thousand Mountains
with Yet/Still, and Other Works

Via Satellite
www.viasatellitemusic.com
Copyright Via Satellite 2019

All rights reserved. No part of this book may be reproduced in any form or by any electronic or mechanical means, including information storage and retrieval systems, without written permission from the author, except in the case of a reviewer, who may quote brief passages embodied in critical articles or in a review. This is a work of fiction. Names, characters, places, and incidents either are the product of the author's imagination or are used fictitiously, and any resemblance to actual persons, living or dead, events, or locales is entirely coincidental.

ISBN: 978-1-939899-33-0

Don't dwell on what was decided before,
or one misses opportunity today.

Only take action on what is front of your eyes.
To plan is a luxury; to dream, a birthright.

Timothy C. Reece
(from *1,000 Loves On Time*)

Dedication

For Timothy C. Reece, our best friend and bandmate.
(May 4, 1977 - May 15, 2017)

Credits

LP / EP

+ =

All songs by Via Satellite
All lyrics by Drew Andrews and Scott Mercado
All performances by Tim Reece, Scott Mercado and Drew Andrews
(except 'Easy', featuring James Trent on bass)
Produced and Mixed by Scott Mercado
Production and Mixing assistance by Drew Andrews and Sven-Erik Seaholm
Mastered by Sven-Erik Seaholm at Kitsch & Sync Production

Main sessions engineered by Sven-Erik Seaholm and Via Satellite at SDRL 01.21-26.2017
Original recording of 'Easy' by Sven-Erik Seaholm at Kitsch & Sync Production, 2003
Additional recordings by Tim Reece, Drew Andrews, Scott Mercado, and Sven-Erik Seaholm
including 'Berlin', 'Gentlemen', 'White Ruins', and 'Harmless, Harmless', 2007
Album Layout and Design By Scott Mercado

BOOK

= +

Artwork by Timothy C. Reece
Layout & Design by Drew Andrews
All writings by Drew Andrews, Timothy C. Reece, and Scott Mercado

Thanks

+-

First, very special thanks to the Reece family for their love, support, and patience.
Forever thanks to Sven-Erik Seaholm for his whole heart on this record & countless others.

Love and thanks to Sarah Longville and Rachel Perez
for hearing these songs over & over again, and still loving us.

Love and thanks to Jen Reece and Dominic Tarantino for everything, everything, everything.

Thank u Brad Lee for years, for SDRL, hosting the party, and donating your time & energy.
Thanks to Brian Espinoza for bringing your drums and laughter.
Thanks to Eric Howarth and Tim Mays @ Vinyl Junkies for their endless dedication to music.
Andy Pates, Jimmy Lavalle, Craig Oliver, Seth Combs, Russel Adams, Adam Gnade, Ben Heywood, Erik Norgaard, Matt Bennett - thank you.

Via Satellite's tenure ended as the labor of three, but other loved and talented friends were members of Via Satellite over the years:

Matthew Reece (founding member/vocals, guitar)
Rod Campbell (founding member/bass)
Paul Mossbarger (guitar)
James Trent (bass)

We treasure you all

Within

Forward
From Drew
From Scott

Part I : A Thousand Mountains

Part II : Yet/Still

Part III: Other Works
Field Manual : Survival Guide
CLIck
A Kubler-Ross Theory
Ghosts in the Black Attic

Discography

Forward : Drew

Over holidays and other visits in from Denver, Tim would summon Scott and I around beers to dream up the next album we would make - *didn't someone have a cabin near Big Bear we could spend a week recording in? Let's do it all sample-based! Make a bunch of loops, send them back and forth digitally, the 'anti-band' band album! Lets see if we could go record in Japan somehow!* On and on and on, year after year, we would toast (making sure to awkwardly make eye contact, as Tim was known to insist on) and agree - this would, for sure, be the year of Via Satellite.

In August of 2016, Tim called to say his body was overcome by an aggressive Stage 4 cancer. He would be entering chemotherapy immediately. With the chemo, he wouldn't survive more than a year or two. Without it - six months or less.

The truth of it all took time to set in, it was impossible. Vegetarian, yoga instructor, a deep connection to his own physicality, the nuance he manifested through rhythm of his drums - something had to be wrong. Not Tim.

Tim's idea (for years) was the right one - we needed to make one last record together. I wanted to take songs I thought were pretty good from a very old live recording of ours called, 'The Kubler-Ross Sessions', re-create them with all new arrangements. Tim wanted to complete our last unreleased songs and yet also to write new material in the studio, and then work on the songs at our own houses and explore new approaches to instruments. Scott agreed in taking scattered songs we had written after our last album, *Cities Are Temples*, and finish the songs we had long delayed finishing, an album Scott had given the working title, 'A Thousand Mountains'.

In the end, we incorporated elements of all these ideas and more. We each dug through our old practice recordings, listened to home studio snippets, unmarked discs, (we found one song with only one known recording from a live show from somebody in a crowd!), listened in to decipher lost lyrics - we searched high and wide, and came back with 25 songs to work with.

14 of those songs were recorded in San Diego beginning on January 22, 2017, the day after Donald J. Trump was (so. fucking. tragically.) inaugurated. It felt like we were back to our fighting ways, all in against the fakes and the fascists, just as alive as ever. Alongside our long-time engineer, my biological father, Sven-Erik Seaholm, we spent five of the very best days of my life, recording the songs presented here. To speak more of it would diminish the utter joy felt inside that studio.

Except for this detail: Tim's mother would drive him to the studio every morning, where he often would seem to fall right out of the car, halfway into his six month chemo treatment, and I would wonder if he could play drums that day, or maybe Scott and I would work on other parts, take it easy and just hang out, whatever Tim wanted to do. Then he would get behind the kit, 100% locked in, with palpable steel and purpose...and keep us there for hours. Every day. Every day, cancer-ridden, holes in his bones, *he would be in it*. He would play and play and play and play. It was the most inspiring thing I have ever seen in a man - watching my best friend charge against the odds. I most truly hope, that my life, in some small way, achieves a greatness like I witnessed.

Tim was my compass and confidant. I am so grateful for Scott, and all who hold us both through. Listen closely and turn this up loud - joyous noise from 3 friends who dreamed / loved / created.

Forward : Scott

A Thousand Mountains

In the face of adversity most people fall apart. They fall to wayside or they simply run away. Others, presented with the same challenges, step up. They toughen. They batten the hatches and turn toward the storm. Such was our Tim and the brothers of Via Satellite.

In the grand scheme of things we were some of the luckiest people to walk the earth. We were young, from stable families, and could afford to make music. But in the pinball machine of music, we didn't exactly have an easy turn. To start with, the industry exploded at our very feet. We had been lucky enough to catch the attention of a few major labels. We even made it to the big tables. But our album was too "arty" and we wouldn't change it. Then Napster happened, people stopped buying cds and, well, you know the rest.

Ok, bands are supposed to tour to make a living. So we buckled up, hit the road, and toured our brains out. And so we did, through broken (yet beloved) vans, blizzards, blazing heat, stolen gear, break downs, accidents, no gas, no money, and well...cough...other problems. Well, ok, that's basically tour. But you get the idea. It wasn't exactly the festival scene in a tour bus. While we did have some bright spots touring with some pretty great bands, and it's great way to see the world, we mostly faced very tough situations. Ok, ok. Never mind all that. Keep making art.

Upside! We were each asked to join our favorite bands (The Album Leaf & The Black Heart Procession among others). Downside! We are no longer in the same city at the same time. Ipods come. Ipods go. Time stretches on. Tours and bands come together. Tours and bands fall apart.

Yet / Still

Via Satellite never stopped being a band. We never stopped making art. And we never stopped being friends. We practiced when we could. We wrote songs from a distance and we played the occasional show. We never stopped trying. Tim wouldn't have it. I don't recall a single conversation with Tim that didn't involve pushing our art forward. Make it. Create it. Change it. Never stop.

On the day Tim told me about his cancer, I learned how resolved he was as an artist. It might as well have been an asteroid coming to destroy the earth. The seven horsemen. He's undeniably stubborn! Tim's words latched around one thing. Art. Let's make the record we've been planning for years. The circumstances don't matter. Let's keep making art.

On January 22nd, 2017, Tim showed up at SDRL in a big black leather jacket. He was frail, wobbly, and somehow a cannonball. He was ready to get started and never ready to stop. Even when his legs gave out, he'd only take a break. Another take. Another song. Something new.

When Drew and I last visited Tim, days before he passed, he was no different. He showed us his newest poetry, his newest paintings, his latest music, and his future plans for all the more. In the face of of a thousand mountains, Tim could not be stopped.

Never stop making art

Part I:

A Thousand Mountains

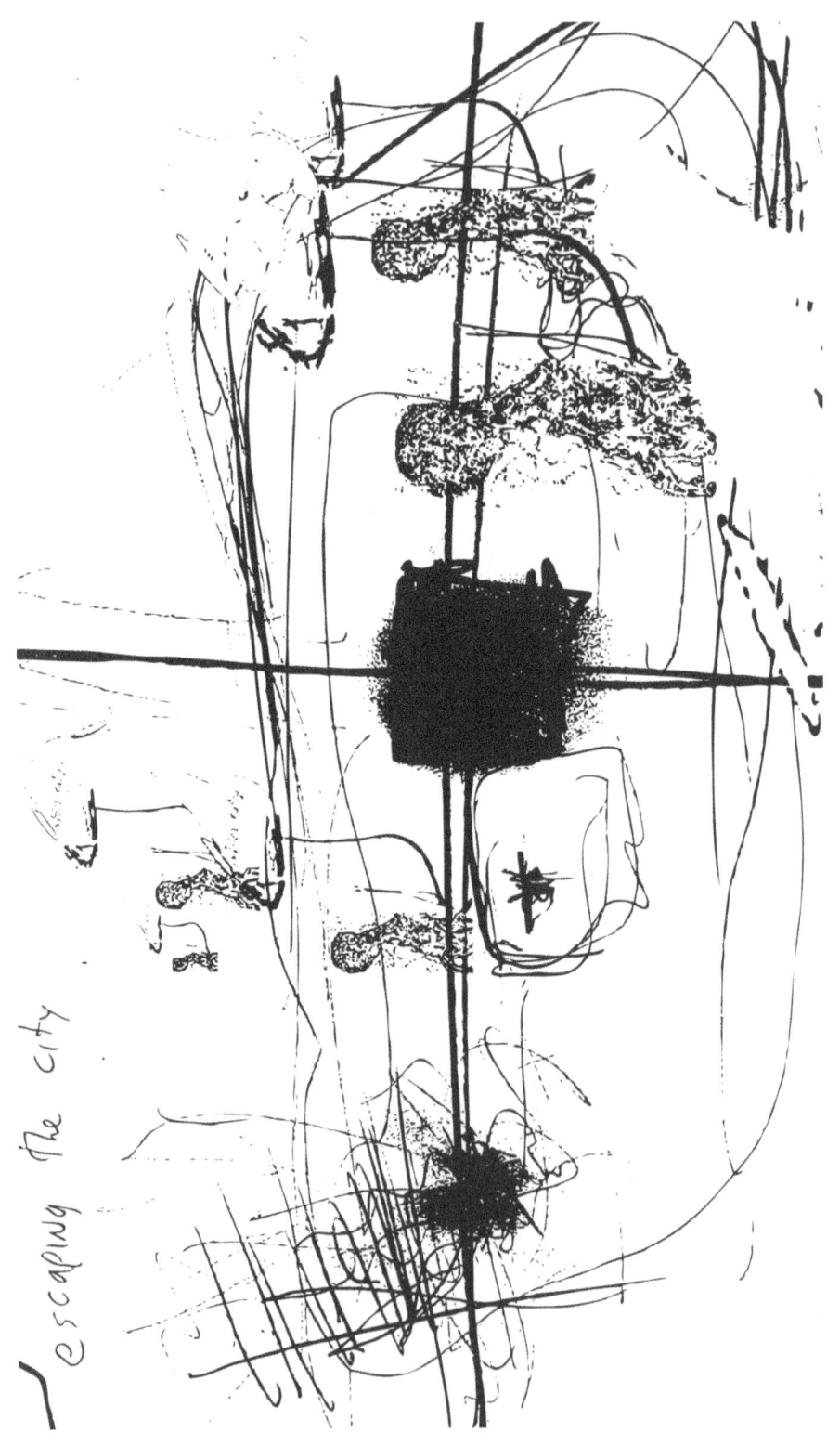

escaping the city

BERLIN

Hardly into daylight, stretched out and torn
Everything you bought you sold
Vacant helicopters, nowhere to go
Wait by the wire and phone

All around the statues, all around Berlin
Black rocketships to set sail again
Every constellation forgotten with Spring
Hundreds of horsemen and hundreds of kings

Try to stop the nightfall, our easy fare
Don't look back to find your home
Can't remember where in hell you have been
Or who you saw, or who set you right here

Silence on the autobahn, everywhere you been
Glass escalators are safe again
Neon lights abide in the center of the stone
Coming for the first and the last of your own

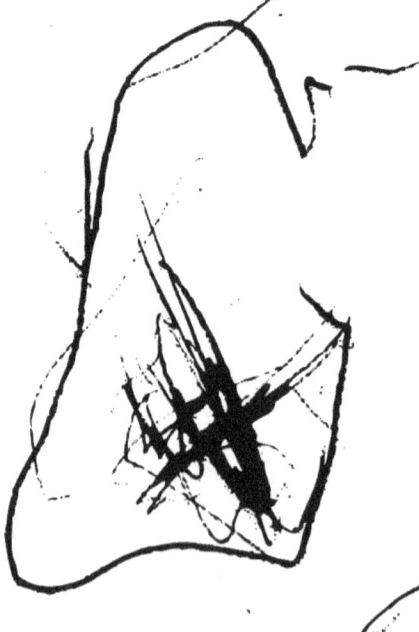

FIRST IN THE MORNING

First in the morning to rise
The constant repair
Always need to reprise what's already there
Though she wants to move on
There's always something wrong

Oh put it into your arms
Oh put it into your lungs
Oh put it into your heart
And you'll find you'll never come back from this
Never come back from this
Know that you'll never come back from this

Tell me you love me

Cry at the end of the song
Always prepared
For the bottom to fall
Never quite there, but you gotta be strong
You've gotta leave Omaha

Oh let it into your eyes
Oh let it into your mind
Oh let it into your heart
And you'll find you'll never come back from this
Know that you'll never come back from this

SEEING THINGS

I can feel the fever
Lie awake and bleed here
Only now fall has come
How much time is left to tell our story

Stuck here waiting for the headlights.
Burn inside. Burn inside out.

We've come so far
To break down the poison and its charms
There's only now. It's beautiful.
The only time that left to tell my story

Stuck here waiting for the sunlight.
Burn inside. Burn inside out.

TALK IT UP WITH GOD

I can talk it up with God
Over radiowaves
Breaking through my static glaze
Tell me what's gone wrong with me?

Hold back your bets to play
To shatter all or fall back
Bend me and feed me words to say
If we learn to talk again

T.V. screens can heal the sick
Everybody's gone plastic
Wrapped in bleach and cellophane
They don't care at all, do they?

Hold back, our words are stained
I blather on, just come back
Fix me, you've got the words to say
If we learn to talk again

If your love moves, tell me it's over
Hearts can steal, tell me it's alright
So still, tell me what's so wrong....

stön building stön traffico

toy soldier

tue	Sven Drw	12—All	o o	ladies AMBO Nopodr zh
wed	Sven Drw	11-40 11-7	o o	Berlin Black lights First
th	Sven Drw	— 11-7	☑ ☑	Gentlemen Haimless the Renefades
F	Sven Drw	11-one	o o	How we Detour Seeing thrn sharks
£			o o	White King inhait the earth
			☐	Twenty Seven

Tg1

	wed	th	
1 · Berlin · Hambs · tou	Gent White Kins inhoit the	AMBO Black 27	Ladies ... 46

1

/with feeling!
/without feeling

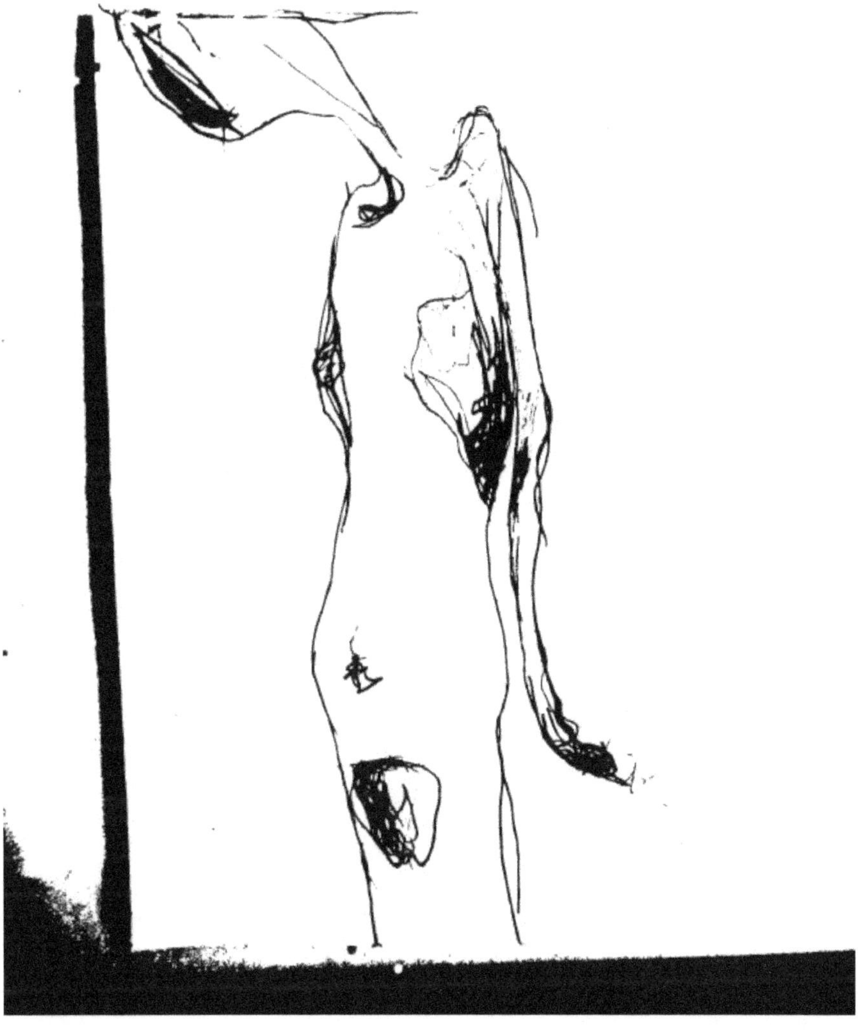

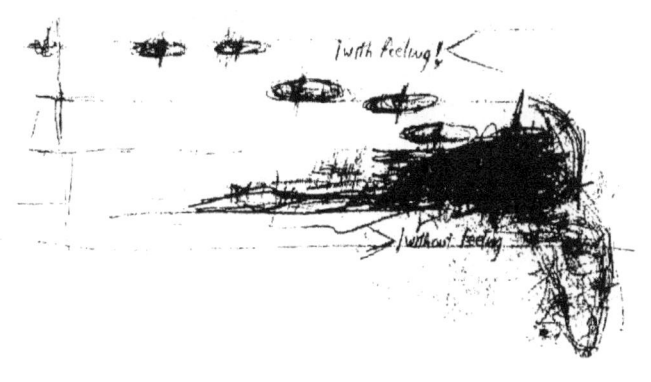

WHITE RUINS

Burn my eyes out overground

Every falsehood, all denial

Cast them out

Lose me in the alley aside

Scratch it off with every landslide

Mountains fall

Unless it is forgotten that we are

All in circles

Believe me that the world is bound to fall apart

Tunnel vision, sand is passing

Don't forget and don't remember

Shut them down

Bury all your charts and tracklights

Take them out to measure faultlines

Watch us up and down again, so lovely and

Unless it is forgotten that we are

All in circles

Believe me that the world is dying to fall apart

Unless it is forgotten who we were

Deep in past times

Believe me that the world is dying to fall apart

i am the beast

i am the boy

i am tired and only 25 **BITTER SOS**

Here's our bitter SOS

Sentimental home address

But we're not moving anything

One more penny left to catch

Just how many will impress

But we're not keeping anything

Better Believe

Bells and whistles, circus tents

Such a pretty one percent

But we're not buying anything

When the lights go out

And the music stops

The day will break

The day will, the day will break

i advance you retreat
i am in love, every day
i am in love

You Better Believe

We're not saying anything

When the lights go out

And the music stops

The day will break

The day will, the day will break

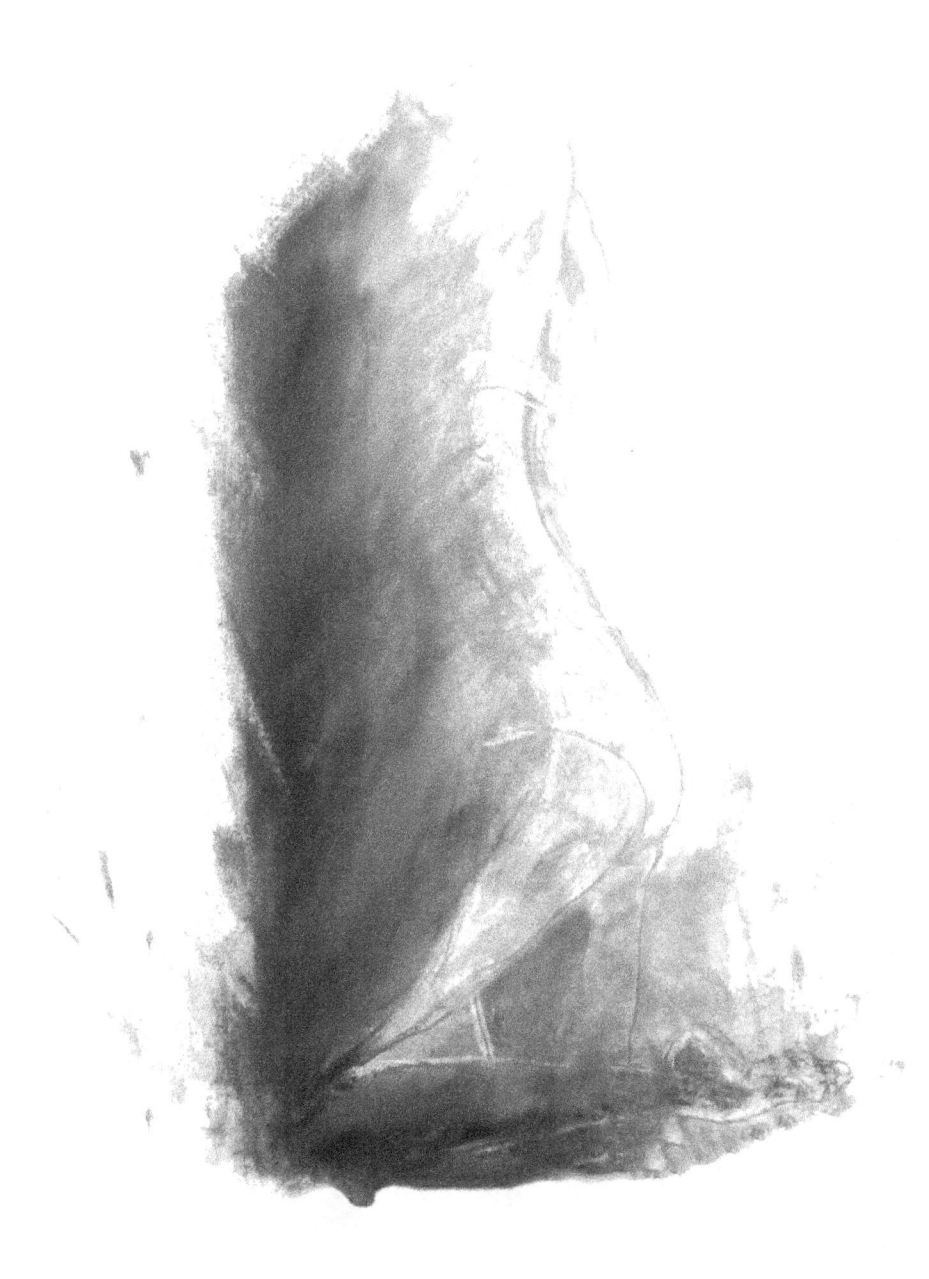

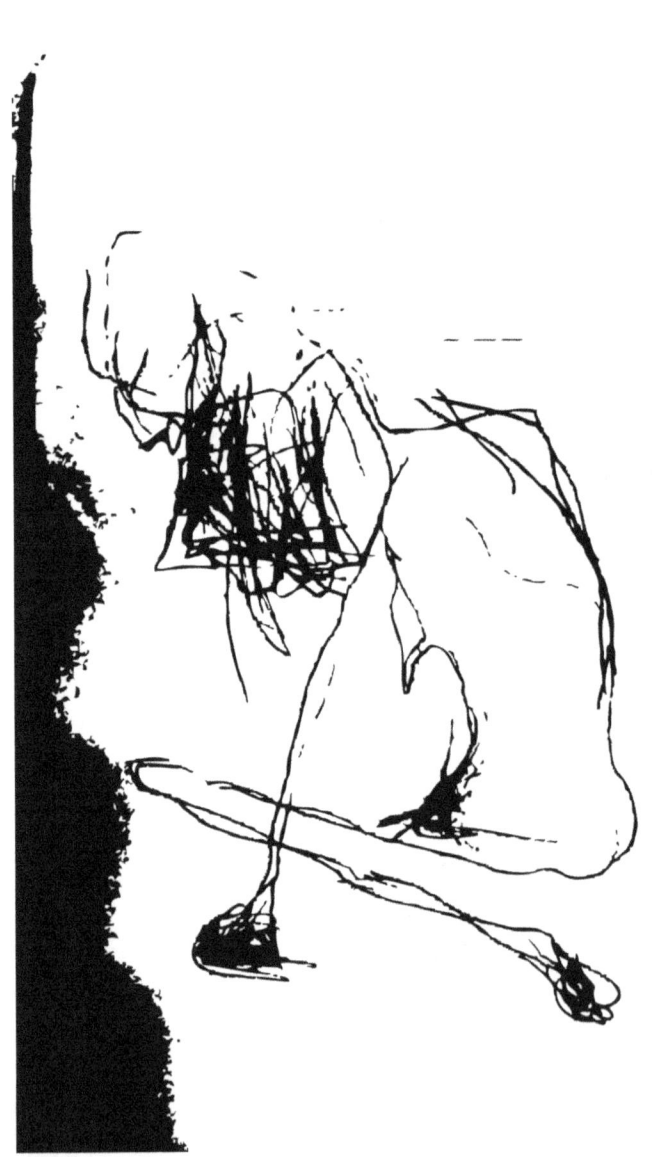

Take 12 - Beginning
Take 13 - V2+C2 (or 11?)
Take 11 - Bridge
Take 13 - Outro

$C^{min} - E^b - B^b - D^{min}/F$

$A^\#, F^\#, C^\#, A^\#, F^\#, F, G^\#$

18711
2.5.3

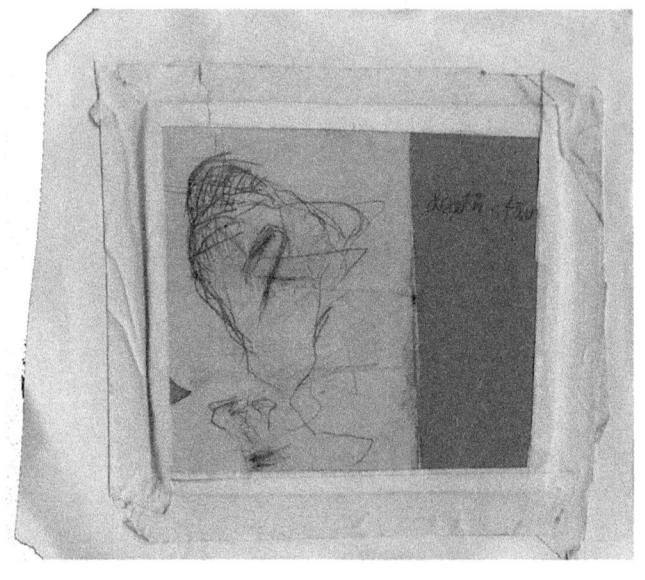

LEVITY

So slowly collapsing
No one could dare to see
Once well over the trees
Now just above the knees

You're leveled
Scaled down

Careful think on your choices
Swear to try real hard
Careful think on your choices
Just never wait too long

So quickly I assume
I'll know just what to do
Once answered with applause
Now left to grasp at straws

You're scared now
Where to?

Careful think on your choices
Swear to try real hard
Careful think on your choices
Just never wait too long

The light in your iris reminds of us God's wrath
The light in your iris reminds us all to laugh
The light in your iris reminds of us God's wrath
The light in your iris

HARMLESS, HARMLESS

Gates, Palaces
Tears you apart
Faith and promises
Sharpen your heart

Hey, you try and carry it all
Hey, why yank the floor out below

Harmless, Harmless, I know
Building rockets, trap doors
In the garden, I know
Reach through the fallout
Day and night

Looking at backwards like it's forward

Planes over you
Lights move below
Faith in cheap wishes
Settle up scores
Hey, stop trying to jump from the car
Vaguely interested
Heart on your arm

Harmless, Harmless, I know
Building rockets, trap doors
In the garden I know
Reach through the fallout
Day and night

This man did not remember the keyword.

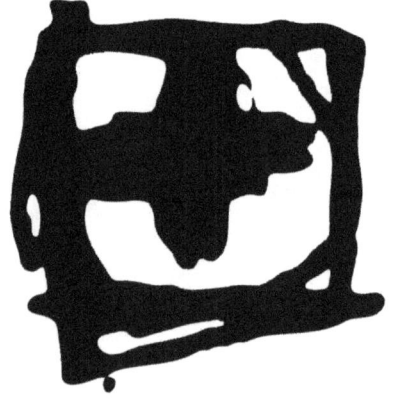

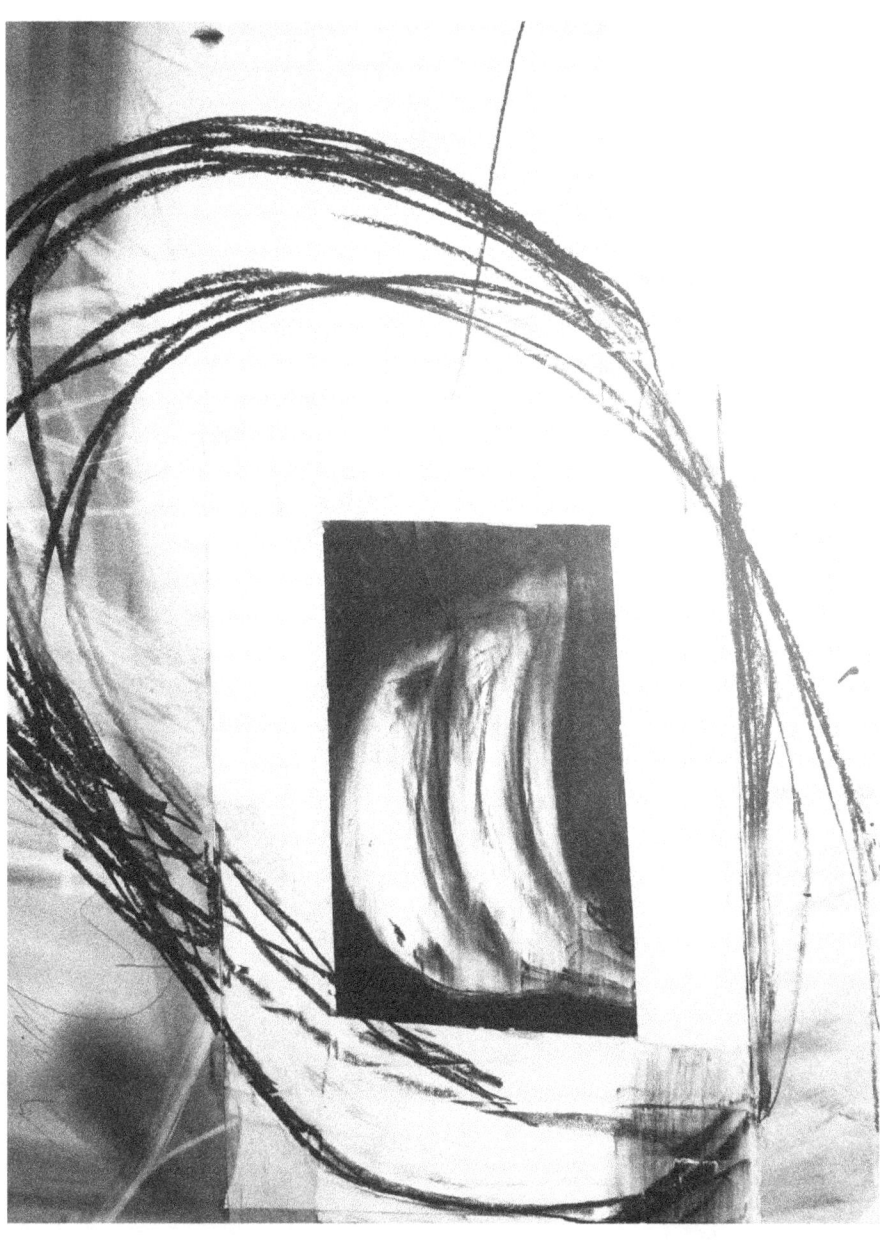

ours is half a heart the killer ate most of the rest

GENTLEMEN

Before you even started
Before you played a part
Before you opened up your heart

The wires had you covered
The fires burned you down
The liars told you who you are

Heavy presentation
At every damned celebration
It's better that I leave now
No salvation
I leave cracks in your foundation
Still I have no weight

Spare your observations
I don't need your confirmation
It's better that you learn now
I'm of vapor
I'm of steam and condensation
And I levitate

Weighs on me
Weighs down on
Weighs on me
Weighs down
Weighs on me
Weighs down on me

How dare you run for cover
How dare you swim for shore
How dare you open up your heart
When all the spirits haunt you
When all senses crow
Each moment hangs there like a gallows
And all the angels highest
And all the angels low
Divide the earth with light and shadow
And all the gentlewomen
And all the gentlemen
Are fighting to be someone they can love

7. BASS DI
8. -TR SCOTT
9. KICK
10. SUB KICK
11. SN TOP
12. SN BTM
13. OH L
14. OH R
15. HH
16. RK
17. FLR
18. ROOM
19. ~~XXXXX~~ GTR
20. - TALKBACK
21
22

21 Keys L
22 Keys R
23 ~~XXX~~
24 DREW LV
25 SCOTT LV
26

1-2	3	4	5	6	7-8
DRUMS	GTR	KEYS	BASS	CLICK	TALK MICS

ponyow

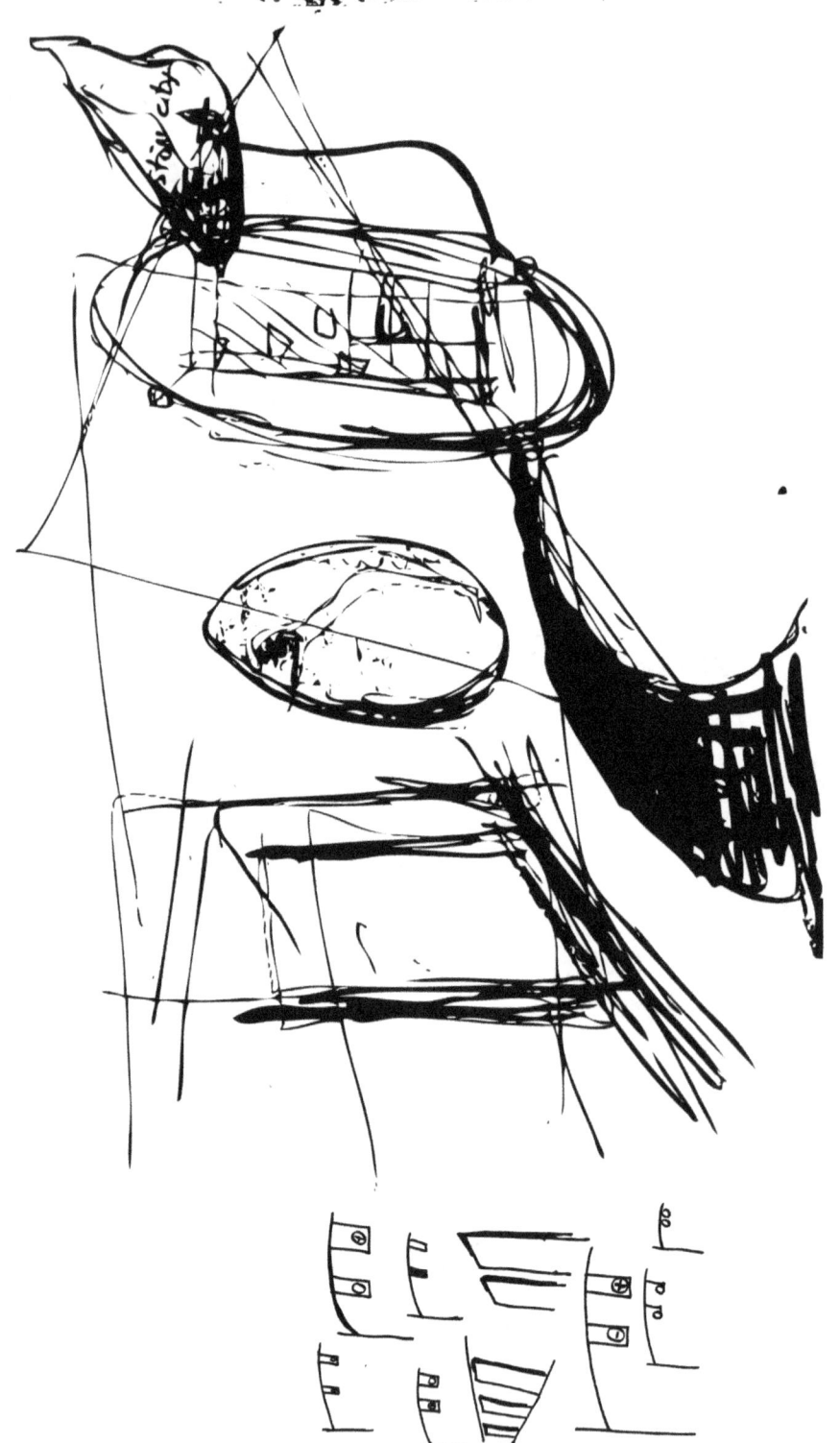

une   quatro

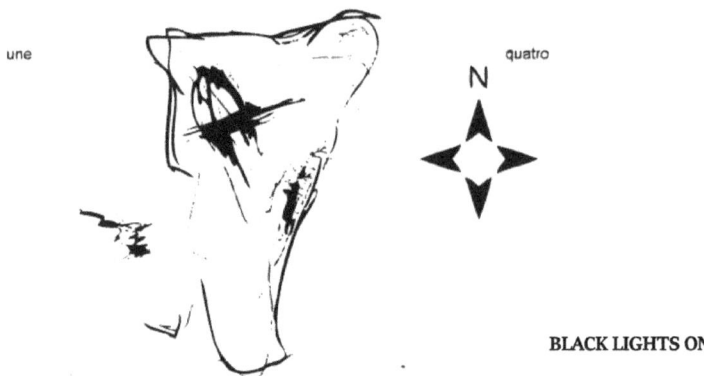

BLACK LIGHTS ON

In the open sky
5 miles from the sun
I'm ready for you to come
Bend to your ear, to whisper what's done
I'm fixing what you've begun

You've been running away all this time
I've seen it all around

In an open field, no reason to fight
I'm dancing with you tonight
Day after year, one thousand mountains
Wait right here to come undone

And you've been running away all this time
But one day we'll embrace our goodbyes
Traffic and tramlines
Waking up heavy
Cities are temples again

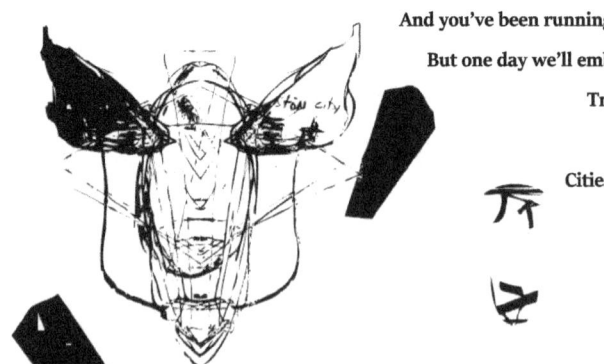

I feel it all around
Black lights on
Black lights on
Black lights on

was asleep for years

~~was asleep~~

Part II:

Yet/Still

EASY

Put me down
There's a reason I live underground
I believe there's a reason light won't shine on me.

I don't know what to say.
(I'm) blind enough to be loved like that
I don't know what to say
Should never stare at the sun

And I know we must be getting somewhere
When summer's out of view
No, we won't be coming back
A shadow of what was there, breaks through

Little doubt
There's a reason she lives in the clouds
Ill-conceived, poor decisions take a shine to me

I don't know what to say.
(I'm) blind enough to be loved like that
I don't know what to say
Should never stare at the sun

And I know we must be getting somewhere
When somewhere is out of view
No, we won't be holding back
A shadow of what was there, breaks through

It's the yellow ones that always throw the shade

Metalanguages of the body

SHARKS

Upside down worlds are coming at me
Ghosts of all your recollection
Everybody lining up to fight me
Kennedys and Rockefellers

Sharks are all around me but I won't be one of those
Punch those greedy bastards in the nose
Sharks are all around me
While I bleed out in the shallows

Grind my teeth with clowns that hang in the deep
What's that noise?
Shadows linger on, they circle round and round and round
No one's here, no one's ever there

Sharks are all around me but I won't be one of those
Punch those greedy bastards in the nose
Sharks are all around me
'Til I wash out in the undertow

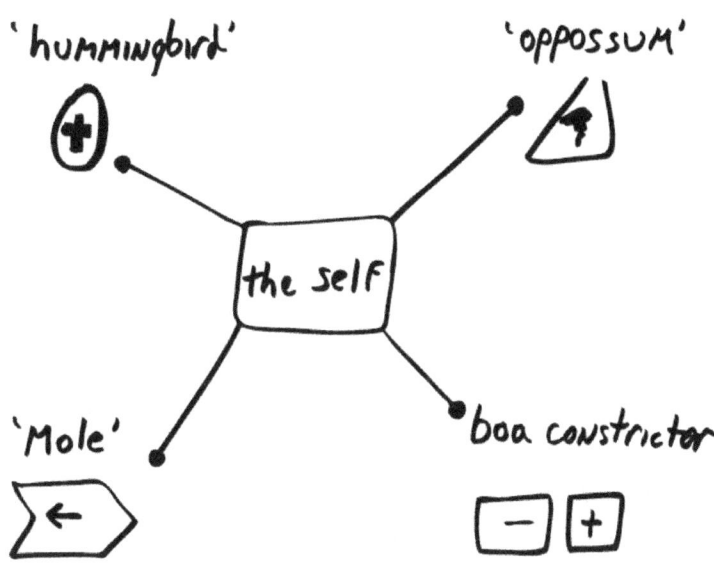
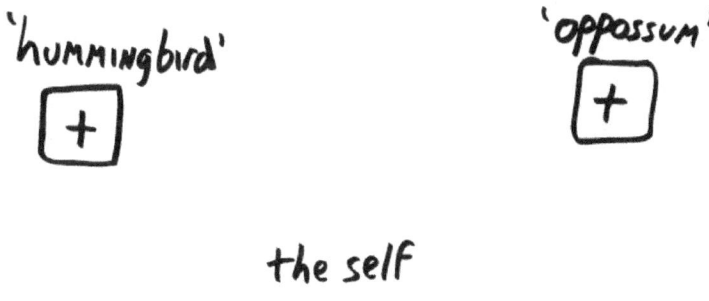

INHERIT THE EARTH

David knocked Goliath down to the ground
Off with his head, everybody was watching
20 feet tall with your fake hair and fake New Yorker's coat
Hack up the facade, send ya back to your Baba

It feels just like walking backwards
But one day
Overthrow you
And I'll inherit this Earth

I stand on your back, dancing down your dirty wall
They come from all sides, yeah, sucka I told you
Ya play with yourself, tiny hands up in your pockets
You're stroking your drones and your ego and your rockets

It feels like walking backwards
But one glorious, most perfect day
Overthrow you
And I'll inherit this Earth

Take back what's left when you leave

David knocked Goliath down to the ground
David knocked that dumb bastard right down to the ground

TRAFFICO

HOT DAMN

Show you're delicate
Say it softly
Every detail reveal

Talk in circles
Swim in signals
Rock and cradle with soft lullabies

So hold me to the coals
Bury me below
I like it when it feels so pure

Lead her gently
And lay your coat down
No more clumsy big mistakes
Get with winning
My head's all spinning
I almost fall asleep, her soft lullabies

So shutter up the doors
Draw 'em into fours
I like it when it feels secure
Like to let you know
Nails across the board
I like it when it feels so lovely

Part III:

Other Works

()

Field Manual : Survival Guide
CLIck
A Kubler-Ross Theory
Ghosts in the Black Attic

()

FIELD MANUAL : SURVIVAL GUIDE
(A public service, brought to you via Via Satellite)

CHAPTER 1

INTRODUCTION

Section I. GENERAL

1. Purpose and Scope

a. Modern living increases the likelihood of your becoming isolated and having to find water, food, and LØVE for many days-even weeks-while making it back to friendly forces. The ability to run from the enemy and to escape LØVE if captured both basic requirements of the consumer's Code of Conduct (sec. 4.4), demands every survival skill you can master. The chances of being exposed are always present, especially when interacting in social situations, so survival techniques should be a part of your basic consumer skills.

b. VIA SATELLITE is a nonspecific organization with nonspecific ideas, culminating in a collection of sounds useful for the brokenhearted (see Cities Are Temples, !TRAFFFICO!, Re:public, Lost Track, Wake Up Heavy). The ideas change and, along with them, the sounds. Sometimes the sounds cannot be identified as such, and begin to take on other identities, electrifying live performances, written words, etc. VIA SATELLITE is an essential component for mastering the survival skills required for maintaining the appearance of social contentment (see Sec. I-1a).

stop or go

Section II. INDIVIDUAL SURVIVAL

1. The Will To Survive

a. If You Are Alone.

The shock of finding yourself isolated, in a plain and disorganized room or in enemy hands can be reduced or even avoided if you remember the keyword:

2. Avoiding Detection

Survival when you are isolated in social situations depends as much on your ability to avoid detection and attachment as it does to find enough food, entertainment, and medication.

pray to Mecca on a street corner

pray to Mecca street corner

You must know:

a. How to conceal your emotions when others are near and how to move without drawing attention to your weakness.
b. The dangers of sudden, rapid movement.
c. How to observe the other without being observed.

a generalized human being

Size up the situation.

3. Suppose You're Captured?
haste makes waste

Remember where you are.
Vanquish fear and panic.

Improvise.

Learn basic skills.
Inside the earth.

outside window

Remember that your friends are
neither your friends nor your enemies—
they are actually disinterested.

\\\

Save pieces of metal no matter how insignificant they may seem.

4. A Plan for Survival

CHAPTER 2
CONTRARY EVIDENCE

Section I. THIS COULD BE YOU

teacher-student

1. Dozen

When you are injured and in pain, it is difficult to control fear. Pain sometimes turns fear into panic and causes a person to act without thinking. One pilot, downed during World War II might have saved himself had he been able to stop and think when his parachute caught in a tree and he was suspended head down, his foot tangled in the webbing. Unfortunately, the pilot's head touched an anthill and biting ants immediately swarmed over him. In desperation he pulled his gun and fired five rounds into the webbing holding his foot. When he did not succeed in breaking the harness by shooting at it, he placed the last shot in his head.

mercy exists in the television and I just keep wanting you to LØVE me that's why when I'm driving alone you spend like a drug but planes still fall from the sky why don't you stay please stay with me please stay with me I couldn't need you more

PLEASE USE THE PRECEDING INFORMATION
IN A RESPONSIBLE AND CONTROLLED MANNER

CLIck

Machines.

They are everywhere.

Full of metal.

Full of little clicks.

They don't talk back.

....909879guf%$#nbfdbi898y .. ..

Not really.

....//..

They connect. Tear apart. Machines can fuck.

They can heal, too. Man creates machines

in reflection of his machine-self.

Man will not survive.

We should all love them.

(text/subtext

How wonderful.

How marvelous.

my ears bleed   from them

the clicking of   the machines

the goddamn   clicking of the machines

make them stop

I fell hard in   love with one.   )))!100001

They fill every   thing, they fill everything.

6442664223226.

When I wake up   I sing to them.

They can't be so   bad.   errorrerso

They hit me ever   now and then.

Nature is a type   of machine.

Birds are   machines.

Crickets,   butterflies,   spiders.

Humans are   little machines

I don't like   to think   about   that.

}{Machines are   the new prophets. The   clicking   of them on   high.

A Kubler-Ross Theory
by Timothy C. Reece

I.

plenty of hours slept in bed. some not in beds. a good amount of cereal eaten. people were met. things were done.

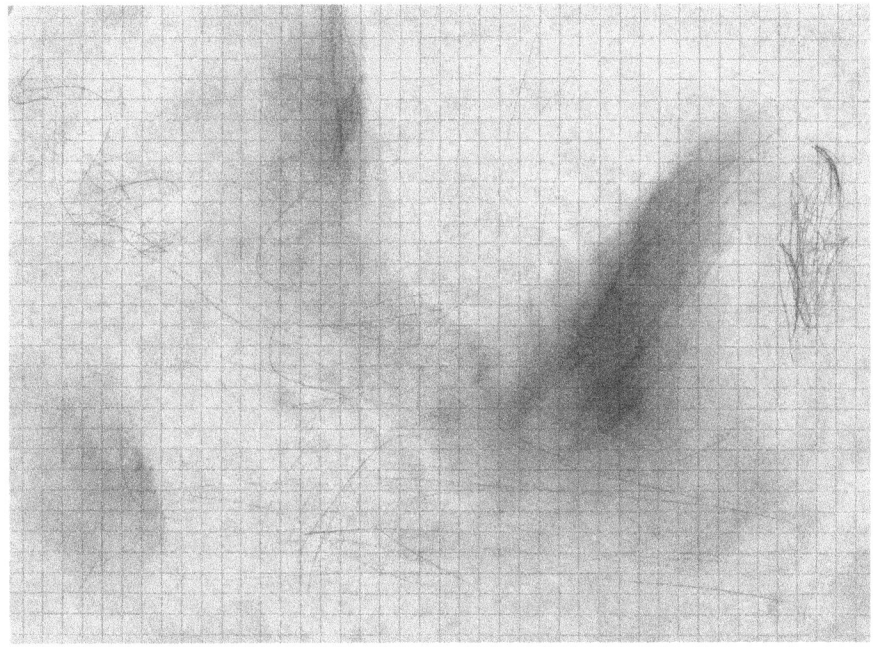

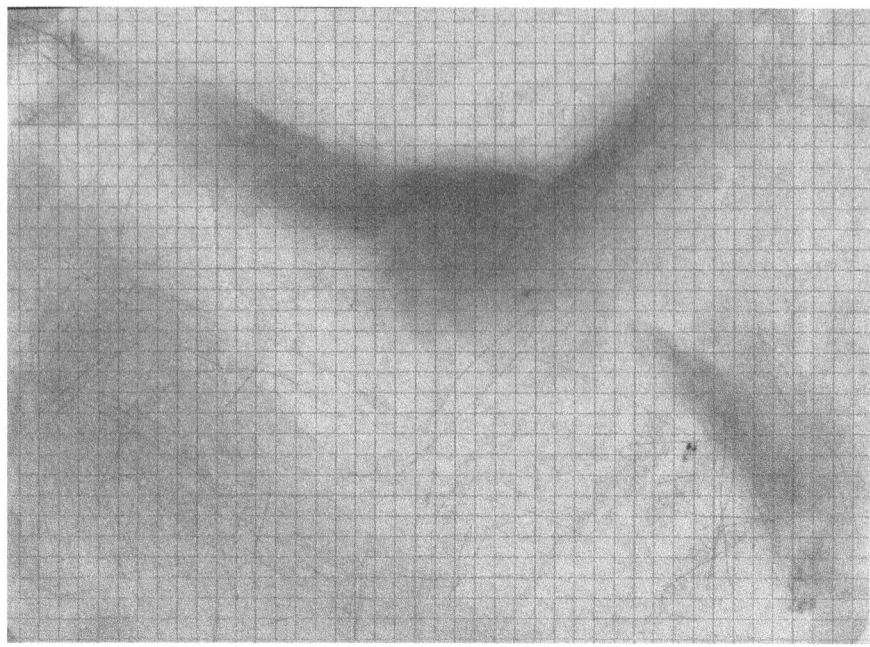

II.

i could not comprehend the particulars of the time. minutes hours days streamed together. yesterday felt like last week. tomorrow seemed like it was always eluding me.

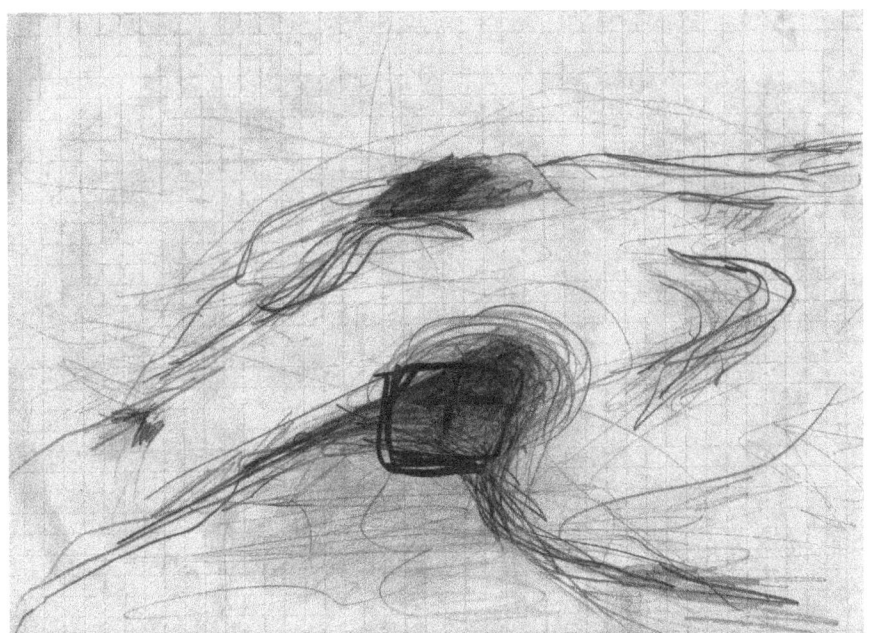

III.

the inside world became monolithic. pillows mock. tableware hurts. words and sentences are like knives in the back of your head.

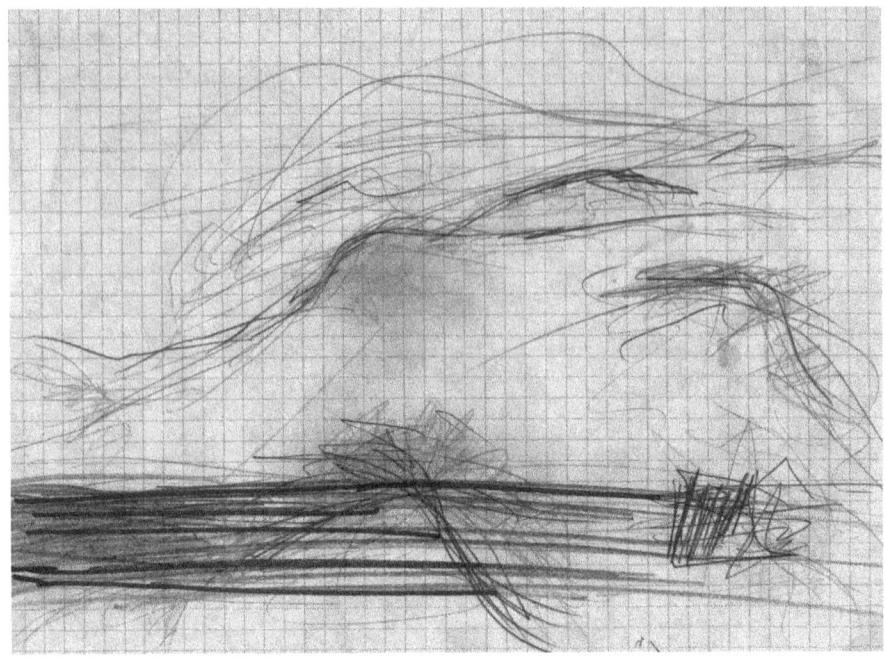

IV.

ordinary things once again take on magical qualities. they have a life of their own. but this time you do not belong to it. you are not included.

V.

a line to your heart.
a story for the afterlife.

Ghosts in the Black Attic
by Drew Andrews

Icy Lake Eerie
Gambling towns entombed under the sheath
Pickaxing twenty miles deep
Seeking skyscrapers and gold zeppelins
Every fine metropolis privy to ballooning

Home. Housing. Under cotton white chill.

In Tampa Bay
The Cubanita is bone frail and unmatched
Whisper in her ear, "Tienes mi corazon?"
"No," she answers. "I have ghosts in the black attic,
And they know you by name."

Belligerent, insides spilled hot off I-10,
Headlight blown, 20 miles outside Lafayette,
Trailer trash taverns lead you astray, deeper into Okonochee Bayou,
Where you pray to St. Christopher of Travels
You never pray anymore
You don't remember the 4-fold suffering or the way of men
There are ghosts in the black attic
They are cataract

Taipei, July, sweat soaked
One-armed wrestler takes the tournament
Weeping and praising unpronounceable gods
You seek them next day at the Lung Shan temple
Casting the divination lips
The wish faulted by the cast lot
The fat monk puts his hand on your shoulder
He says, "There are ghosts in the black attic, They recite the Gospel of John endlessly"

They are sorry in Munich for the choice of your country. "Maybe the next president, maybe he then is better, I like Americans anyway."
Days later in Koln, lost,

Anxiety attacks throw you to the street.

More seizures will come, you contemplate what it means to die.

You no longer fear hell. You fear the rising sun.

Five belly bikers on Harleys will lead you home.

Mary Kay sales women keep the way.

There are ghosts in the black attic

They may pencil you in

ARCO Oklahoma City

Where hath your spirit gone

Emptied to the drop cans of Tecate

Exhaled out in clouds at the gas pumps

Once again to ether sky, your truest house

Stifled by the wired hum in the aorta, swallowed Xanax

The lilting flurry of oak out the thumbsmudged window

Deaf in an ear and telephoned in the other

Filing through streets of Vienna

Ferry cafeteria on the Balkan Sea, wanting

Forgotten - how it went down

Who and when you are where how did it why

In the cold ring wash, in the strobe trembled calves,

In sketched out thinking

Overcome seizure with Buddhist technique learned in Osaka

Where is your spirit

Tattooed cattle gone, forest of lifeless smoky maple.

Fishing ware out of Wal-Marts and Texas roadhouses off I-35,

A visitor drunk in wartime.

What her name was is gone with your spirit.

In the carnival, 12 years old, kissing on the YMCA Ferris wheel, her name

Emergency blinkers of Mack trucks.

Bottled water from the Ozarks.

First Millennial Tabernacle of Seven-Winged Lions.

Gulf thunderstorm and Midwest snowstorm.

Where hast your spirit

The greased hair of no days of wash
There are ghosts in the black attic
They have all the answers

Under banana shrub, muggy North Carolina, deconstructing
Southern writers. In a moment, eyes and wolves.
That old friend is alcoholic, you say, let's go home.
The genteel applaud, both your teeth grow, roommates
cupped against old Victorian doors. Home a couch,
you fall to each other, both shy and salty from rainpour.

They fill everything
All these ghosts, weep weep weep

Lower East Side Manhattan
Chicano peddlers chanting "Si, lo siente,"
A festival en memoriam Ginsberg our Lord
Whom seateth enthroned
Levis wared for ten bucks
Geisha slippers five less
With guitars pawned by junkies last night for twenty
The rock and roll singers
Less than you earn on Saturday night
The rock and roll singers
Wait wait wait wait wait wait wait wait

In the Bronx with dropouts, we were the same and not the same.
In Brooklyn with barbers, we all were found.
In Queens, voodoo women signing,
THERE ARE GHOSTS IN THE BLACK ATTIC
AND SMOKE GETS IN THEIR EYES

Empty lost alone misplaced spent worn down whittled
Faintly hearing sleigh bells

I am with you

the room
The room
the room
The room
the room
The room
the room
the room
the room
the room

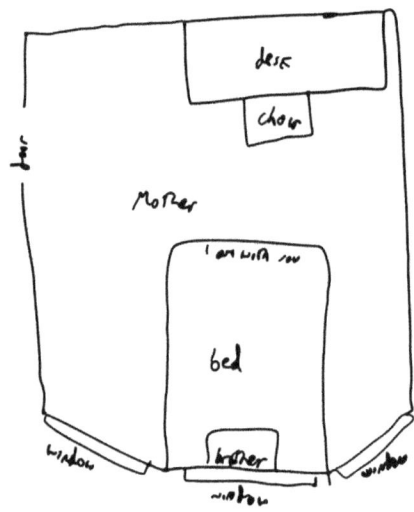

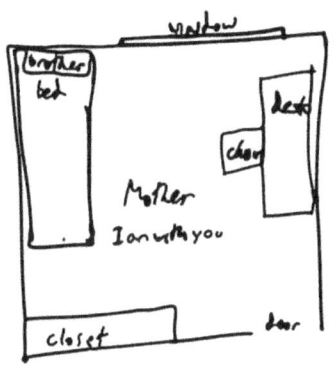

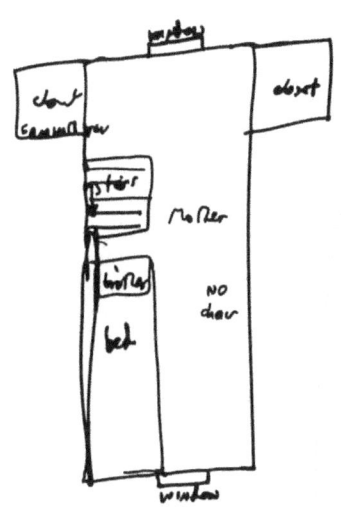

mother - room
brother - pillow
J - chair
an - desk
with - picture
you - lamp

Officer Smith outside of Yuma
20 bucks of weed, sparkly red Chinatown bag
Prison court on 2nd St. and 1st Ave
14 bills 14 hundred dollar bills
Inmates next to you chained, their breath
Elaine Emorick twitch without amphetamines
Jose Ruis go to jail two nights
Mr.A. 14 Franklins 14 hundred dollar bills
Mugshot fingerprint put your belongings here
Strip search (you high?) the minimum the maximum
There are ghosts in the black attic
Repeat offenders and Calypso dancers

Under the frozen lake an apartment
After the thaw, a home for you
Dig deeper and find it, hurry come on

Red wooden floors. Black Siamese cats.
Snow on the tenement. Project on project.
Cabbies swerving. Ambulances barrel.
Vomit urinal. Orange traffic uniforms bubbling.
The lifted. The brokenhearted. Icicle eaves.
Maple trees. Lady Liberty.
Snowbanks. Air filters. Codes. 4 way crossings.
White poppies. Telephone wire. John Deere. Seashells.
(slow down slow down wanderer)
We should go now. Crows in Tokyo. Karaoke.
Tamami. Chiake. Chelsea. Kicking through the powder.
Lost the numbers. Harrison police. Thick fern. Exit 24.
The cherry blossom. Cigarette and laundromat.
(slow down slow down wanderer)

Gated communities in the water. Old choice. Many problem. Holy temple.
Holy old ghosts. Videographers. London fog. Wolf River Railway.
There are ghosts in the black attic
They have no idea

Diana the psychic

In five years you will have none of the same friends

Money is nowhere in your future

Do what you love

Do what you love

Do it for love

Restless ghosts, undone spirits

Miss Blondie, exotic dancer,

Calls you honky cracker whiteboy,

Face bruised from her muggy meat breasts and crushed cans of Pabst Blue Ribbon

For days, contemplating, what do old dancers do when their bodies collapse to cancer

And no woman or man will have them

And no tax will cover their ragged clits

Gone to Portland, Kyoto, Kansas City, Copenhagen

Railroad track ghosts lay in Baton Rouge, Louisiana

Skirting the banks of the Mississippi

Arms wingspread like Lord Jesus on the balance beam

You walk on singin' old Gospel songs sung in Vacation Bible School

You smoke cigarettes and meditate on the Lamb's Book of Life

5th grade summer camp staring at the moon, repenting

You were a slave too

Then freed

Then made a slave to whom freed you

Then freed again

Now a slave to Jameson and collapsing hours

The crawdad boil starts at 4:45

Time will be broken in the last days

There are ghosts in the black attic

Kneeling in aisle 7

Hunting an eighth in Seattle

Your ex calls her coke dealer who tosses cats off the balcony,

Who has Adderall and Neurontin and Klonopin

You just want weed

Nobody likes me in there, he says.

No, come in. We like you.

You just want to smoke a joint, Marcus shot a man, confessing to you,

You're like a priest, he says, I can trust you, I like you,

I shot a man. You should be a minister.

Quiet when his .45 slips to the carpet,

Open those eyelids, lift high those exalted eyes

Put away your rosaries

Champagne and Swiss ballet

Hopping balloons in Berlin

Filming high debutantes of Krakow

Where are you

Quiet temples in Kyoto of wax and apples

Dirty South club beat in Atlanta

Pesos tossed to beggars under bridges in Mexico

Open blue of the Tyrrhenian

There are ghosts in the black attic

Sharks, mimes, women at the market

Croatian men shooting basketballs into trash cans, the hours

Cursing all presidents on the White House lawn, the hours

Suffocating in caves, audience, the hours

It is not good for man to be alone

Sleep with easy ghosts

3 a.m. is colder in the North

In Toronto, Stockholm, Cambridge,

Halloween girls wear the bone tight skirt

Stalking the gutters, all fathers

Giggling in taxis

Masquerade high-rise spa

Poison ghosts abound with the moth

2 of afternoon is siesta in Spain

People eat snails of the sea and drink the beer of Five Stars

Usted no entiende como cuál debe estar libre

There are the ghosts in the black attic

That hide, spin their wheels and were there at the Fall

All roads flow to the Pacific,
All streams empty up the 80 overpass,
All children love mother, fathers in the wing,

Shattering mirrors on the blacktop in Tucson
Where is it
Beard buried in Shinjuku
What wind has carried the spirit
Medicines confiscated Chicago customs
What false god beckons
Lay down in the Colosseum
Hear them singing

There are indeed ghosts
Without discernible hymn
Violets, alibis, endless rivers

THE (END)

DISCOGRAPHY

*

Please Play This Music (1999)
Wake Up Heavy (2000) *
!TRAFFICO! (2001)
re:Mix (2003)
We Heart Music (split EP w/Goodbye Blue Monday) (2003)
Cities Are Temples (2004) **/***
Lost Track (2009)
Yet/Still (2019)****
A Thousand Mountains (2019)****

*Pseudocool Records
**Loud and Clear Records
***Human Highway Records (Japan)
****500 Records (digital) / Vinyl Junkies (vinyl)

Re: Via Satellite

Via Satellite formed in 1999, and began recording it's final album in Jan 2017.

Comprised of drummer Tim Reece, singer/multi-instrumentalist Drew Andrews, and singer/mulit-instrumentalist Scott Mercado, the band has recorded many full-length albums and EPs together.

-Connect-

web: viasatellitemusic.com
bandcamp: viasatellite.bandcamp.com
facebook: facebook.com/viasatellitemusic

www.ingramcontent.com/pod-product-compliance
Lightning Source LLC
Chambersburg PA
CBHW031450070426
42452CB00037B/436